READING/WRITING COMPANION

Mc
Graw
Hill
Education

Cover: Nathan Love, Erwin Madrid

mheducation.com/prek-12

Send all inquiries to:
McGraw-Hill Education
Two Penn Plaza
New York, NY 10121

ISBN: 978-0-07-901848-9
MHID: 0-07-901848-3

Printed in the United States of America.

7 8 9 LMN 23 22 21   B

Welcome to Wonders!

Read exciting **Literature**, **Science**, and **Social Studies** texts!

★ **LEARN** about the world around you!

★ **THINK**, **SPEAK**, and **WRITE** about genres!

★ **COLLABORATE** in discussion and inquiry!

★ **EXPRESS** yourself!

my.mheducation.com

Use your student login to read core texts, practice grammar and spelling, explore research projects and more!

GENRE STUDY **1 REALISTIC FICTION**

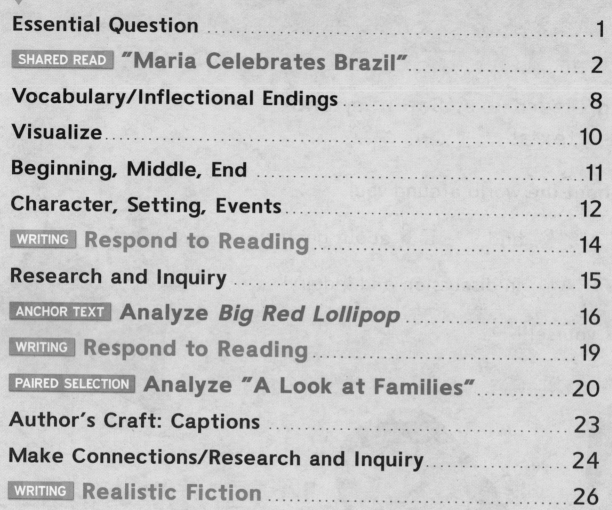

GENRE STUDY 2 FANTASY

GENRE STUDY 3 EXPOSITORY TEXT

SOCIAL STUDIES

WRAP UP THE UNIT

SOCIAL STUDIES

Talk About It

Unit 1 • Realistic Fiction

COLLABORATE

In some places, families celebrate a spring holiday called Holi. They use powder to show the colors of blooming flowers.

Talk with a partner about what is happening in the picture. How are your family celebrations the same? How are they different? Write your ideas on the chart.

SOCIAL STUDIES

Same	Different

TAKE NOTES

Asking questions helps you figure out what you want to learn, or your purpose for reading. Write your questions here.

_____

_____

_____

_____

As you read, make note of:

Interesting Words _____

_____

Key Details _____

_____

_____

_____

Maria Celebrates Brazil

Essential Question

? How are families around the world the same and different?

Read about a family from Brazil.

Maria and her family are in their bright, hot kitchen. "Please, Mãe, por favor!" Maria begs.

Mãe speaks Portuguese. This is the **language** of Brazil. "No matter how much you beg or **plead**, you must go to practice. The parade is next week."

FIND TEXT EVIDENCE

Read

Paragraph 1

Character, Setting, Events

Draw a box around the characters. Where are they?

_____

_____

_____

Paragraph 2

Beginning, Middle, End

Circle what Maria's parents want her to do in the beginning of the story.

Reread

Author's Craft

Why does the author use Portuguese words in the story?

FIND TEXT EVIDENCE

Read

Paragraphs 1-3

Beginning, Middle, End

Circle what Maria says about going to practice. **Draw a box** around the reason she feels this way.

Paragraph 4

Visualize

Underline details that help you picture the parade. What can the family share there?

_____

_____

Reread

Author's Craft

How does the author use dialogue to show the way each character feels?

"It's not **fair**," says Maria in English.

Mãe does not know a lot of English. Maria is surprised when she asks, "What is not fair about going to practice? You must do the right thing."

"Ana **invited** me to her house," Maria answers. "I want to go!"

Pai says, "Maria, the parade is important. People from around the world come to see it. They try our food, see how we dress, and how we live. It is a chance for us to **share** our **culture**."

"I know but I really want to see Ana," says Maria.

Pai says, "Maria, you can see Ana another time. They are giving out costumes at practice today."

Maria thinks about her father's words. Pai is right. She and the other children have worked hard for a year. They practiced their dance steps over and over. They even made their own bright colorful costumes.

FIND TEXT EVIDENCE

Read

Paragraphs 1-2

Character, Setting, Events
Draw a box around what Maria can do another time. What important **event** is happening today?

_____

_____

Paragraph 3

Inflectional Endings
Circle the ending added to _practice_. **Underline** what the children did over and over to do it better.

Reread

Author's Craft

Why does the author describe Maria's thoughts?

FIND TEXT EVIDENCE 🔍

Read

Paragraph 1

Beginning, Middle, End

How does Maria feel about going to practice now?

_____

_____

_____

Paragraph 2

Character, Setting, Events

Underline the two sentences that tell when and where the parade takes place.

Reread

Author's Craft

Why does the author use an illustration to support details about the setting?

"You're right," Maria says to her father. "I'll go to practice. I'll tell Ana I cannot visit her."

One week passes. Lots of people line the streets. The children in Maria's group are wearing their sparkling costumes. They know each dance step. They dance to the beat.

The crowd moves **aside** as they make their way down the street.

When the crowd moves away, Maria sees a woman with a camera. She is hurrying. The woman **scurries** by Maria. She puts her camera to her eye. Maria smiles from ear to ear. She is excited to be in the parade. Click! The woman takes a picture of Maria. Maria is proud of her hard work!

Summarize

Use your notes and think about the events in the beginning, middle, and end of "Maria Celebrates Brazil." Summarize the important events.

FIND TEXT EVIDENCE

Read

Paragraph 2

Visualize

Circle the person Maria sees when the crowd moves away. **Underline** details that help you picture what the character is doing.

Beginning, Middle, End

How does Maria feel about going to practice at the end of the story?

_____

_____

_____

Janet Broxon

Vocabulary

**Talk with a partner about each word.
Then answer the questions.**

aside

Mia moved **aside** to let her brother pass.

Why do you move aside on a sidewalk?

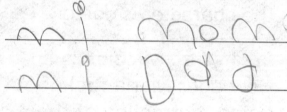

culture

A parade in February is part of the
culture of Brazil.

What is an important event in your culture?

_____

Build Your Word List In your
writer's notebook, write a definition
for an interesting word you picked on
page 2. Use a dictionary to help you.

fair

We are **fair** and treat everyone the
same.

What is one way to be fair at school?

_____

_____

invited

We **invited** the school to watch our
play.

Tell about an event you were invited to.

_____

_____

language

My friend speaks more than one
language.

What language do you want to learn?

_____

_____

plead

My little brother will **plead** with me to play with him.

What is something you might plead for?

_____

_____

scurries

The squirrel **scurries** up the tree.

What other animal scurries in nature?

_____

_____

share

I will **share** my orange with my friend.

What is something you can share with a friend?

_____

_____

Inflectional Endings

To understand the meaning of a word, you can separate the root word from the ending, such as *-ed* or *-ing*.

🔍 FIND TEXT EVIDENCE

I'm not sure what hurrying *means. To hurry means to "move quickly." The ending* -ing *can mean "something happening right now." I think* hurrying *means "moving quickly right now."*

Maria sees a woman with a camera. She is hurrying.

Your Turn Use the endings to figure out the meaning of the word below in "Maria Celebrates Brazil."

wearing, page 6 _____

_____

Janet Broxon

Visualize

When you visualize, you use the author's words to form pictures in your mind about a story.

🔍 **FIND TEXT EVIDENCE**

When you read the last sentence on page 5, use the author's words to help you visualize the costumes.

Page 5

Maria thinks about her father's words. Pai is right. She and the other children have worked hard for a year. They practiced their dance steps over and over. They even made their own bright colorful costumes.

I reread, "They even made their own bright colorful costumes." I can picture in my mind the bright colors of the costumes. This helps me visualize what their costumes are like.

Your Turn Reread the second paragraph on page 6. What details help you picture the parade and Maria's group of dancers?

_____

_____

Beginning, Middle, End

"Maria Celebrates Brazil" is a realistic fiction story. The characters, settings, and events are made up, but they could really happen. A realistic fiction story has a beginning, a middle, and an end.

FIND TEXT EVIDENCE

I can tell that "Maria Celebrates Brazil" is realistic fiction because the characters, settings, and events could be real. The story has a beginning, middle, and end.

Readers to Writers

Writers organize stories with a beginning, middle, and end. A story with three clear parts helps readers follow the main events and understand the characters. You can plan a story you write in this way.

Page 4

"It's not **fair**," says Maria in English.

Mãe does not know a lot of English. Maria is surprised when she asks, "What is not fair about going to practice? You must do the right thing."

"Ana **invited** me to her house," Maria answers. "I want to go!"

Pai says, "Maria, the parade is important. People from around the world come to see it. They try our food, see how we dress, and how we live. It is a chance for us to **share** our **culture**."

Beginning, Middle, End

In the beginning of the story, Maria wants to skip practice and go to a friend's house. Her parents remind her why practice is important.

Your Turn How does the author show Maria's feelings about going to practice change in different parts of the story?

_____

_____

_____

Janet Broxon

Character, Setting, Events

A character is a person or an animal in a story. The setting of a story tells when and where a story takes place. The events are what happens.

 FIND TEXT EVIDENCE

As I read pages 2 and 3 of "Maria Celebrates Brazil," I learn who the characters are, where the story begins, and what the characters are doing.

> **Quick Tip**
>
> The setting is important because it helps you to understand the characters and events. Look at the chart. Dance practice takes place one week before the parade. This explains why Maria's parents want her to go.

Character	Setting	Events
Maria Mãe Pai	The family's kitchen one week before the parade	Maria tells her parents she wants to miss dance practice. Her parents want her to go to practice.

COLLABORATE

Your Turn Continue rereading the story. Fill in the information in the graphic organizer about the characters, settings, and events. Then talk with your partner about an example of why the setting is important.

Character	Setting	Events
Maria Mãe Pai	The family's kitchen one week before the parade	Maria tells her parents she wants to miss dance practice. Her parents want her to go to practice.

Respond to Reading

COLLABORATE

Talk about the prompt below. Think about how the author shows what is important to Maria and to her parents. Use your notes and graphic organizer. Try to include new vocabulary in your response.

How does the author show that family members work together to make good decisions?

_____

_____

_____

_____

_____

_____

_____

Internet Search Using Keywords

Keywords will help you find facts quickly. Keywords are important words you use when talking or writing about a topic. When you do an Internet search, keywords tell the search engine what to look for.

Imagine you want to find information about family celebrations in Brazil. What keywords could you use?

_____

_____

Make a Poster With a partner, make a poster that shows how foods are the same and different around the world. You could focus on:

1. one kind of meal, such as breakfast.

2. one kind of food, such as bread.

3. the most popular foods from different countries.

What is your topic? _____

_____

Discuss the keywords you can use for your Internet search.

What do people eat for breakfast in France? What keywords can the author type into a search engine to find the answer?

_____

_____

Big Red Lollipop

? How does the author show the way Rubina feels when Sana and Ami do not understand her problem?

Literature Anthology: pages 10–31

COLLABORATE

Talk About It Look at the illustration on page 12. Talk with a partner about how you think Rubina feels.

Cite Text Evidence Write clues from the text and the illustration where the author shows Rubina's feelings.

Clues from the Text	Clues from the Illustration

Rubina's Feelings

Combine Information

Look back at page 11. Why is going to a birthday party important to Rubina? Use text evidence to support your response.

Write The author shows Rubina is feeling _____

_____

_____

? **How does the author use an illustration to help you understand the way Rubina feels toward Sana in the middle of the story?**

Talk About It Look at the illustration on pages 20–21 of the **Literature Anthology**. Talk about what it shows.

Cite Text Evidence What clues from the text and the illustration help you understand how Rubina feels?

Clues from the Text	Clues from the Illustration

Write The text and illustration help me understand that

_____

_____

_____

Quick Tip

As you read, use these sentence starters to talk about how Rubina feels.

Rubina compares her sister to...

Rubina's face looks...

Make Inferences

Why does Rubina use the word "rat" to describe how quickly Sana moves?

? **How does the author help you understand Rubina's traits?**

Talk About It Reread page 28. Talk with a partner about what Rubina thinks and does.

Cite Text Evidence Complete the chart with what Rubina thinks and what she does when her sister is invited to a party.

What Rubina Thinks	What Rubina Does

Write The author helps me understand that Rubina is

_____

_____

_____

Quick Tip

Authors use words and illustrations to describe the traits of characters. Some traits describe how a character looks, such as tall. Other traits describe things about a character that you cannot see, such as brave.

Make Inferences

Why do you think it is difficult for Rubina to do the right thing?

Respond to Reading

COLLABORATE

Discuss the prompt below. Think about how the author shows Rubina's thoughts and feelings in different parts of the story. Use your notes to respond to the prompt.

How does Rubina's relationship with her sister Sana change from the beginning of the story to the end?

_____

_____

_____

_____

_____

_____

_____

_____

Quick Tip

Use these sentence frames to organize your text evidence.

At the beginning of the story, Rubina feels...

At the end of the story, Rubina feels...

Self-Selected Reading

Choose a text. Read the first two pages. If you don't understand five or more words, choose another text that will let you read for a longer amount of time. Fill in your writer's notebook with the title, author, genre, and your purpose for reading.

A Look at Families

Families around the world do some things the same. They have differences, too. Let's take a look at how families in different cultures live.

All families need homes. Some families live in large cities. They might live in tall apartment buildings. Many families live in the same building.

Literature Anthology: pages 32–35

Reread the first paragraph. **Underline** two sentences about families around the world. What will you look at as the text continues?

_____

_____

Reread paragraph 2. **Draw a box** around what all families need. **Circle** details that tell about where some families live.

COLLABORATE

Talk with a partner about how people in large cities may live. Use the details in the text and the photograph to support your ideas.

©Kentaroo Tryman/Johner Images RF/age fotostock

Some families live near water.
Some families live in houses on stilts.
Stilts are tall poles. They keep the
homes safe from water.

Reread the paragraph. **Draw a box** around the author's definition of stilts. Look for the stilts in the photograph.

Why do some families live in houses on stilts? **Underline** the text evidence. Write your answer here.

_____

_____

_____

COLLABORATE

Ask and answer questions about the different kinds of homes people live in around the world. Support your ideas with details from pages 20–21. You may also make connections to your own experience or to other texts you have read.

Paul Taylor/The Image Bank/Getty Images

? **Why does the author tell about families from many parts of the world?**

Quick Tip

The author shows that families have the same needs and activities around the world. Make connections between the families you read about and your own family.

Talk About It Reread pages 32–35 in the **Literature Anthology**. What does the author tell us about families?

Cite Text Evidence Write details from the text that show how all families are the same.

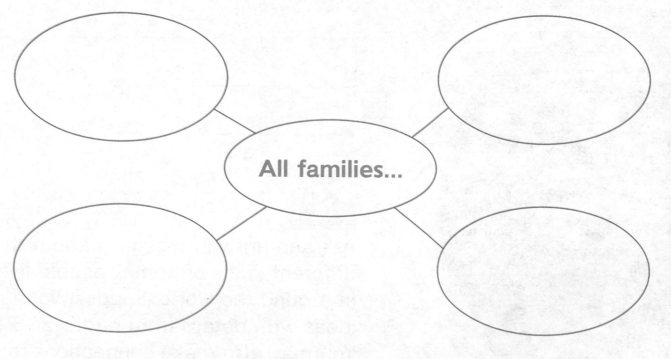

All families...

Write The author wants to explain that _____

_____

_____

blue jean images/Getty Images

Captions

Captions are words that tell about a photo, map,
or other text feature. Authors use captions to give
information about what appears in the text feature.

FIND TEXT EVIDENCE
Look back at the photographs and captions on page 32
in the **Literature Anthology**. What did you learn from
the captions?

_____

_____

_____

Your Turn Look back at the photos and captions on
page 33. How do the captions help you to understand
the purpose of these photographs?

_____

_____

_____

? What have you learned from the selections and song about friends and families doing things together?

Talk About It Read the song. Talk about what the song says about being with friends. How is this like being with family?

Cite Text Evidence Circle a clue from the song that tells you how friends are like family.

Write This song and the selections I read help me

understand that _____

_____

_____

_____

_____

_____

_____

Quick Tip

Use these sentence starters to talk about friends and families:

Friends are like family because...

My family spends time together...

The More We Get Together

The more we get together, together, together

The more we get together, the happier we'll be.

For your friends are my friends, and my friends are your friends,

The more we get together, the happier we'll be.

— German Folk Song

Present Your Work

With your partner, plan how you will present your poster to the class. Use the Presenting Checklist to help you improve your presentation. Discuss the sentence starters below and write your answers.

An interesting fact I learned about foods around the

world is _____

_____

I would like to know more about _____

_____

Expert Model

Literature Anthology
pages 10-31

Features of Realistic Fiction

Realistic fiction is a story that could happen in real life.

- The characters act and speak like real people.

- The narrator uses words that tell sequence, or the order of events.

- The story has a beginning, middle, and end.

Analyze an Expert Model Studying *Big Red Lollipop* will help you learn how to write realistic fiction. Reread page 25. Answer the questions below.

How do you know that time has gone by in the story?

_____

_____

How does the author show that Sana has a problem?

_____

_____

_____

Plan: Brainstorm

Generate Ideas You will write realistic fiction about a family. Use this space for your ideas. Draw and brainstorm words that describe the characters, setting, and events you might write about.

Shutterstock/bogdan ionescu

> **Quick Tip**
>
> As you brainstorm, think about a problem a family member might have or an event that can make family members feel closer.

Plan: Choose Your Topic

Writing Prompt Write realistic fiction about a character in a family. Show how the character's feelings change. Complete these sentences to get started.

My characters are _____

At the beginning of the story, _____

_____

In the middle, _____

_____

At the end, _____

_____

 Purpose and Audience Some authors write realistic fiction to entertain their audience. They may also want to show how people learn and grow. Think about why you chose your characters. Then explain the purpose for writing your story in your writer's notebook.

andresr/E+/Getty Images

Plan: Organization

Develop Sequence Authors think about the order, or sequence, of events in a story. Read the chart below. Write *first*, *next*, and *last* to show the sequence of events.

Quick Tip

Some words and phrases help show that the story is moving from one part to the next. You can use words like *first, later, then, after that, when, finally,* and *in the end.*

_____, the backyard gate is open. Annie's puppy is gone!

⬇

_____, Mom and Dad help look for Daisy. They hear a bark.

⬇

_____, they see Annie's friend Gina. She is holding the puppy! "Daisy wanted to visit my yard," Gina laughs.

Plan In your writer's notebook, make a chart like the one above. Fill it in with details about what happens at the beginning, middle, and end of your story.

Draft

Descriptive Details The author of "Maria Celebrates Brazil" uses details to describe the characters and setting in the beginning of the story.

> Maria and her family are in their bright, hot kitchen. "Please, Mãe, por favor!" Maria begs.
>
> Mãe speaks Portuguese. This is the language of Brazil. "No matter how much you beg or plead, you must go to practice. The parade is next week."

Use the paragraphs as a model to start writing. Think about details that describe your setting. Include descriptive details in the words your characters speak.

_____

_____

_____

Write a Draft Look over the chart you made. Use it to help you write your draft in your notebook. Remember to use details that describe, or tell about, your characters, settings, and events.

Revise

Strong Openings A strong opening grabs your attention and makes you want to find out what happens next. Read the story opening below. Then revise it. Add details about the character and his problem to make readers interested in the story.

Tim had slept late. He needed to make a picnic for Father's Day.

Outside his bedroom window, there were clouds.

_____

_____

_____

_____

Revise It's time to revise your draft. Include a strong opening that makes your reader want to find out what happens next.

Quick Tip

Strong openings can describe a problem a character faces, or has, in the story. Think about details that show what the character feels about the problem. Dialogue, or what a character says, can show strong feelings.

Grammar Connections

Pay attention to your end punctuation marks. Use question marks at the end of questions. Use exclamation marks when you write sentences that show a strong feeling.

Revise: Peer Conferences

Review a Draft Listen carefully as a partner reads his or her work aloud. Begin by telling what you liked about the draft. Ask questions and make suggestions to give the writer ideas for making the writing stronger.

Partner Feedback Write one suggestion that you will use in the revision of your story.

Based on my partner's feedback, I will _____

_____

_____

After you finish giving each other feedback, reflect on the peer conference. What was helpful? What might you do differently next time?

_____

_____

Revision Use the Revising Checklist to help you figure out what text you may need to move, add to, or delete. Remember to use the rubric on page 35 to help you with your revision.

Remember to use the rubric on page 35 to help you with your revision.

Quick Tip

Use these sentence starters to discuss your partner's work.

I enjoyed your story opening because...

How about adding details about...

I have a question about...

Revising Checklist

☐ Does my story fit my purpose and audience?

☐ Does it include descriptive details?

☐ Does it have a strong opening?

☐ Does the story have a beginning, middle, and end?

Edit and Proofread

When you **edit** and **proofread**, you look for and correct mistakes in your writing. Rereading a revised draft several times will help you catch any errors. Use the checklist below to edit your sentences.

Grammar Connections

When you revise your writing, make sure that you capitalize the first word in every sentence. Be sure to use the correct end punctuation for all of your sentences.

✓ Editing Checklist

☐ Are all sentences complete sentences?

☐ Do all questions end with question marks?

☐ Do sentences that show strong feelings, such as excitement, end with exclamation marks?

☐ Do statements end with periods?

☐ Are all the words spelled correctly?

List two mistakes you found as you proofread your story.

1 _____

_____

2 _____

_____

Publish, Present, and Evaluate

Publishing Create a clean, neat final copy of your story. You may add illustrations or other visuals to make your published work more interesting.

Presentation Practice your presentation when you are ready to present your work. Use the Presenting Checklist to help you.

Evaluate After you publish and present your story, use the rubric on the next page to evaluate your writing.

1 What did you do successfully? _____

_____

_____

2 What needs more work? _____

_____

_____

✔ Presenting Checklist

- ☐ Sit up or stand up straight.
- ☐ Look at the audience.
- ☐ Speak slowly and clearly.
- ☐ Speak loud enough so that everyone can hear you.
- ☐ Answer questions using details from your story.

Listening When you listen actively, you pay close attention to what you hear. When you listen to other children's presentations, take notes to help you better understand their ideas.

What I learned from ....'s presentation:

_____

Questions I have about ....'s presentation:

_____

✓ Listening Checklist

☐ Make eye contact with the speaker.

☐ Listen for details about characters.

☐ Listen for details about a beginning, middle, and end.

☐ Identify what the speaker does well.

☐ Think of questions you can ask.

4	3	2	1
• tells a lively, realistic fiction story about a character in a family • begins with a strong, detailed opening • has a clear beginning, middle, and end • is free or almost free of errors	• tells a story about a character in a family • begins with a strong opening • has a beginning, middle, and end • has few errors	• tries to write realistic fiction but details are unclear • lacks a strong opening • makes an effort to sequence events and create a beginning, middle, and end • has many errors that distract from the meaning of the story	• does not focus writing on the genre or topic • lacks an opening • does not sequence events into a beginning, middle, and end • has many errors that make the story hard to understand

Talk About It

Essential Question

How do friends depend on each other?

COLLABORATE

These friends are using a map. They are helping each other find out where they are on the map. There are many ways we depend on our friends.

Talk with a partner about how friends depend on each other, or help each other. Then write your ideas on the web.

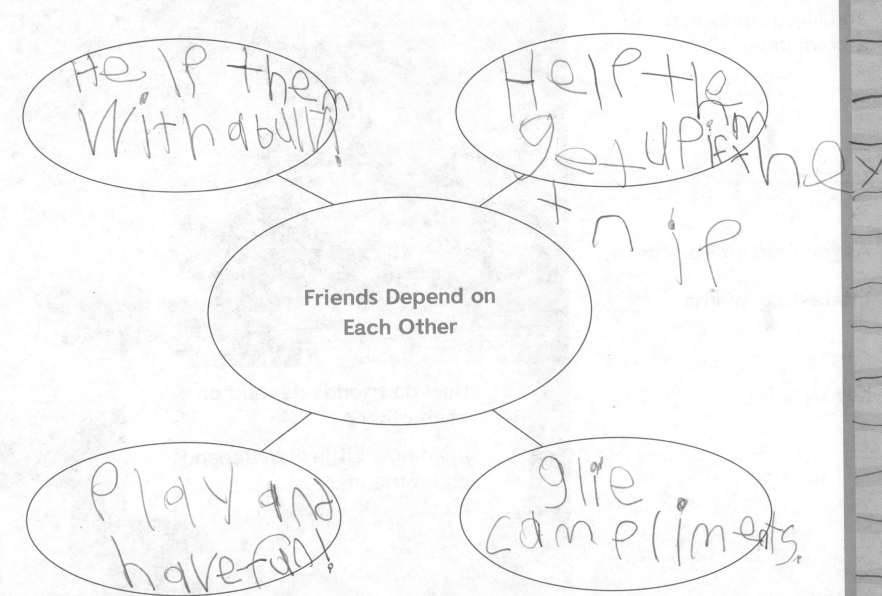

Help them With a bully!

Help the get up if they trip

Friends Depend on Each Other

play and have fun!

give compliments.

TAKE NOTES

A prediction is a guess about what will happen in a story. Use the title and illustrations to make a prediction.

_____

_____

_____

As you read, make note of:

Interesting Words _____

_____

Key Details _____

_____

_____

_____

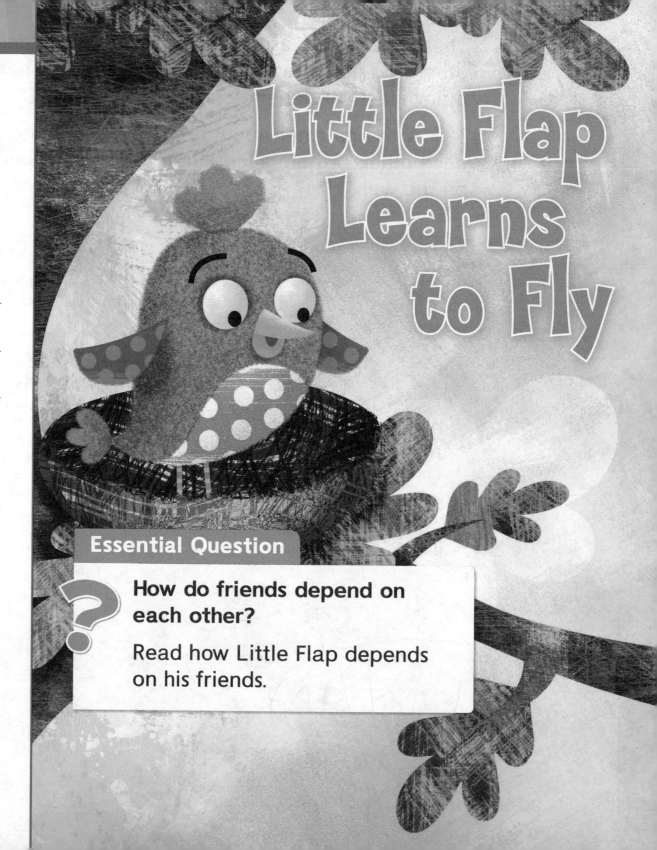

Little Flap Learns to Fly

Essential Question

? How do friends depend on each other?

Read how Little Flap depends on his friends.

Little Flap was happy living in his nest. His friends, Fluff and Tuff, lived in the nest next to him. Every morning they sang songs together. Their parents brought them worms to eat.

One day Fluff asked, "Can we get our own worms?"

Tuff said, "We can if we learn to fly."

Fluff said, "Yes! Let's learn to fly."

Tim Beaumont

FIND TEXT EVIDENCE

Read

Paragraph 1

Visualize

Draw a box around details that help you visualize why Little Flap is happy living in his nest.

Paragraphs 2-4

Key Details

Underline what Fluff wants to get. What must the little birds do first?

learn to fly

Reread

Author's Craft

How does the author use dialogue to show what the little birds want to do?

FIND TEXT EVIDENCE

Read

Use Illustrations

What does Little Flap look like? Use the illustration to describe his traits.

_____

_____

Paragraphs 2-3

Key Details

Circle why Fluff wants the birds to practice flapping their wings. What do Tuff and Little Flap do?

_____

_____

Reread

Author's Craft

What details help you understand the way Little Flap feels?

Little Flap **peered** over the edge of his nest. It was very high up. When he looked down, the ground seemed very far away. He felt scared! He was too **afraid** to tell his friends about his fear so he kept his feelings a **secret**.

Fluff said, "Let's practice flapping our wings. It will make them strong. Watch."

Tuff and Little Flap watched Fluff. Then they copied her **actions**.

Soon it was time to fly. Little Flap could no longer keep his feelings a secret. He asked, "Will I fall? I don't want to get hurt."

Tuff said, "You can **depend** on Fluff and me. We're your friends."

Fluff said, "I have an idea. We will go first and show you how. Then you can try. If you fall, Tuff and I will **rescue** you."

Tuff said, "Yes, we can save you!" Tuff and Fluff jumped out of the nest. They flew!

Little Flap looked down **nervously**. He still felt uneasy, but he felt braver with his friends. "Okay," he said. "Let's try!"

Tim Beaumont

FIND TEXT EVIDENCE 🔍

Paragraph 1
Root Words

Find the word *asked*. **Circle** the word without the ending *-ed*. **Circle** the question Little Flap asks.

Paragraphs 2-4
Key Details

Underline Fluff's idea. How can Little Flap depend on his friends?

_____

_____

_____

Reread
Author's Craft

How does the author use dialogue to show the birds are good friends?

FIND TEXT EVIDENCE

Read

Paragraph 1

Visualize

Underline words that help you visualize the actions the birds do together.

Paragraphs 3-4

Key Details

Circle what Fluff and Tuff tell Little Flap. Why do they say these things?

_____

_____

_____

_____

Reread

Author's Craft

How does the author show Fluff and Tuff's excitement?

The three birds stood together on the branch. They counted, "One! Two! Three!" Then they flapped their wings fast and jumped. Little Flap lifted into the air.

"You're flying just right!" said Fluff.

"You're flying **perfectly!**" said Tuff.

All three little birds landed in a patch of soft, green grass.

Little Flap said, "Now I know I can always depend on you, Fluff and Tuff! You are my friends."

Then he found a big, juicy worm and shared it with his friends.

Now Little Flap likes flying!

Summarize

Summarize "Little Flap Learns to Fly." Then talk about your prediction on page 38. Use the illustrations and title to help you explain why your prediction was correct or needed to be changed.

FIND TEXT EVIDENCE

Read

Paragraphs 1-2
Key Details
Underline the sentence that describes the birds' safe landing. **Circle** what Little Flap then says.

Paragraph 3
Make Inferences
How does the author show that Little Flap is a good friend to Fluff and Tuff?

_____

_____

_____

Fluency

Take turns reading the page aloud. How does the author help you express Little Flap's feelings?

Tim Beaumont

Vocabulary

Talk with a partner about each word.
Then answer the questions.

actions

The girl's actions helped her team win.

What actions help you do well in school?

paying attton to the teacher

afraid

Our dog is afraid of thunder.

What is something you are afraid of?

I am of mi mom is

Build Your Word List Choose an interesting word that you noted. Look up the word's meaning and pronunciation using a dictionary online.

depend

Nick and Maria depend on Dad to help them learn to ride a bike.

How do you depend on family members?

love

nervously

Maya waited nervously for her running race to begin.

What did you wait nervously for?

a shot

peered

The dog peered through the hole in the fence.

What did you see when you peered out of the classroom window?

playground

perfectly

The ball is **perfectly** round.

What is something that is perfectly flat?

_____

_____

rescue

We saw the boy **rescue** the cat from the tree.

What is another word for rescue?

_____

_____

secret

Mandy whispered a **secret** to me.

What is special about a secret?

_____

_____

Root Words

To understand the meaning of a word you do not know, try to separate the root word from an ending, such as *-ed* or *–ing*.

🔍 **FIND TEXT EVIDENCE**

I'm not sure what landed *means. I'll split the root word* land *from the ending* –ed. Land *can mean "to move down onto the ground." The ending* –ed *means this action happened in the past. So,* landed *means "moved down onto the ground."*

All three little birds landed in a patch of soft, green grass.

Your Turn Use the root word to figure out the meaning of another word in the story.

jumped, page 41 _____

_____

Visualize

When you visualize, you form pictures in your mind about the characters, setting, and events in the story.

🔍 **FIND TEXT EVIDENCE**

After reading page 40 of "Little Flap Learns to Fly," I know Little Flap is thinking about flying. What words does the author use to help readers visualize the nest?

Page 40

Little Flap peered over the edge of his nest. It was very high up. When he looked down, the ground seemed very far away.

I read that the nest "was very high up" and the ground "seemed very far away." From these details, I can visualize the nest.

COLLABORATE

Your Turn Reread page 43. What words help you visualize where the birds land?

_____

_____

_____

Use Illustrations

"Little Flap Learns to Fly" is a fantasy story. It is a made-up story with characters who could not be real. Often fantasy stories have illustrations that show the characters, setting, and events.

🔍 FIND TEXT EVIDENCE

I can use what I read to know that the story has made-up characters that could not be real. This story is a fantasy.

Page 38

Little Flap Learns to Fly

Essential Question

How do friends depend on each other?

Read how Little Flap depends on his friends.

Illustrations

In this illustration, I see Little Flap wearing clothes. I know birds in real life do not wear clothes. This must be a fantasy story.

COLLABORATE

Your Turn Use illustrations to help you find an event that could not happen in real life. Tell why this story is a fantasy.

_____

_____

_____

Key Details

You can find important information in a story by looking for key details in the illustrations and the text.

🔍 **FIND TEXT EVIDENCE**
As I read page 40 of "Little Flap Learns to Fly," I can look at the illustration and read the text to find a key detail about the characters and events.

Detail
Little Flap is afraid to fly.

Your Turn Continue reading the story. Does Little Flap learn to fly? Use your notes to help you list the key details in your graphic organizer.

COLLABORATE

Tim Beaumont

Detail

Little Flap is afraid to fly.

Detail

Detail

Tim Beaumont

Respond to Reading

COLLABORATE

Talk about the prompt below. Think about important details the author shows in the text and illustrations. Use your notes and graphic organizer.

How does the author show that Little Flap can depend on his friends?

_____

_____

_____

_____

_____

_____

_____

_____

_____

Ask Questions

To learn about a topic, **ask questions** about what you want to know. Sometimes you can talk to people to find answers to your questions. This is called informal inquiry.

You are going to research the topic of how friends depend on each other. What questions can you ask classmates about a time they depended on a friend?

_____

_____

_____

"We Depend on Friends" List In a small group, ask and answer questions about how we depend on friends. Take notes on the answers. Together, create a list of each group member's response. Illustrate the list with a picture.

You will answer questions and tell information. Write ideas about an event that you will tell the group.

_____

_____

Help! A Story of Friendship

? **What does the dialogue at the beginning of the story tell you about Mouse and Hedgehog?**

Literature Anthology: pages 36–57

COLLABORATE

Talk About It Reread pages 37–38. Discuss the dialogue, or what Mouse and Hedgehog talk about.

Cite Text Evidence Write about what the two characters say about Snake.

Mouse Says	Hedgehog Says
snakes are dangerous	snake's your friend

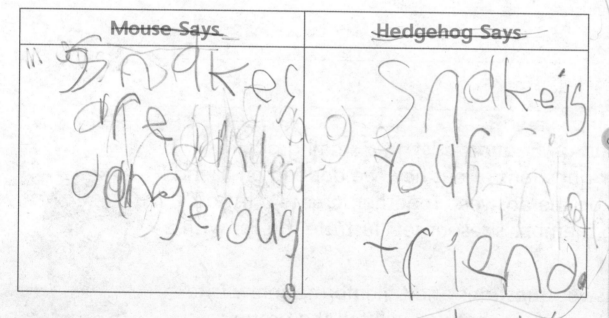

Write The dialogue helps me understand _how friend help eochother._

How does the author show Mouse's feelings after he is rescued?

COLLABORATE

Talk About It Reread page 51. Talk about what Mouse says and does.

Cite Text Evidence What details on page 51 tell you the way Mouse feels? Write the text evidence.

Detail 1	Detail 2

Write I know the way Mouse feels because _____

_____

_____

? **How does dialogue and an illustration show that Mouse is thankful and no longer afraid?**

Talk About It Reread pages 54 and 55. Talk about what Mouse says on page 54. Discuss what the illustration shows on page 55.

Cite Text Evidence Fill in the chart with details that help you understand how Mouse feels.

Quick Tip

Details that tell what Mouse does or show how he looks can help you understand his feelings.

Detail	Detail	Detail
He says thank you.	I picked some flowers for im	Thetd are hugging

Write I know Mouse is thankful and no longer afraid because he ___hugshnim.___

Theme

A folktale's theme is the main message the author wants to tell readers. An author often uses what the characters do and say, or dialogue, to show a theme.

FIND TEXT EVIDENCE

The author uses what the villagers say on page 56 to show why they want to help. The dialogue shows the theme about why people should work together.

> "Let us help you!" they cried. "Many hands make light work."

 Your Turn Talk about what the farmer says in the last paragraph on page 57. How does the author use the farmer's words to show why people should work together?

_____

_____

_____

_____

Quick Tip

The narrator of "The Enormous Turnip" does not tell the theme. But the author shows that working together is important from what the characters do and say.

MAKE CONNECTIONS

? What have you learned from the selections and the painting about the different ways friends depend on each other?

Talk About It Look at the painting. Talk about what the girls are doing. Discuss different ways they may depend on each other.

Cite Text Evidence Circle the clues from the painting and caption that show what the girls are doing together.

Write The selections I read and the painting all show

_____

_____

_____

_____

_____

_____

_____

Quick Tip
Describe what the girls are doing and how they feel using these sentence starters:
The girls are...
The girls look...
They help each other...

This painting is called *Breton Girls Dancing, Pont-Aven,* by Paul Gauguin.

Present Your Work

COLLABORATE

With your partner, plan how you will present your "We Depend on Friends" list to the class. After all the presentations are finished, discuss the sentence starters below and write your answers.

I enjoyed learning about

_____

_____

_____

I think a good friend is a person who _____

_____

_____

_____

We Depend on Friends

Jenny: Marco brought my school work when I was sick.

Nick: Louis made a card for my birthday.

Vicki: Joe helped me when I fell.

✔ **Presenting Checklist**

☐ Hold up your work so that everyone can see it.

☐ Speak clearly.

☐ Point to the part of the list you are talking about.

Talk About It

Essential Question

What happens when families work together?

This family is working together to make a dessert. Working together gets chores done and can be fun! There are many ways families work together.

Talk about what is happening in the picture. Discuss how your family works together. Write your ideas in the web.

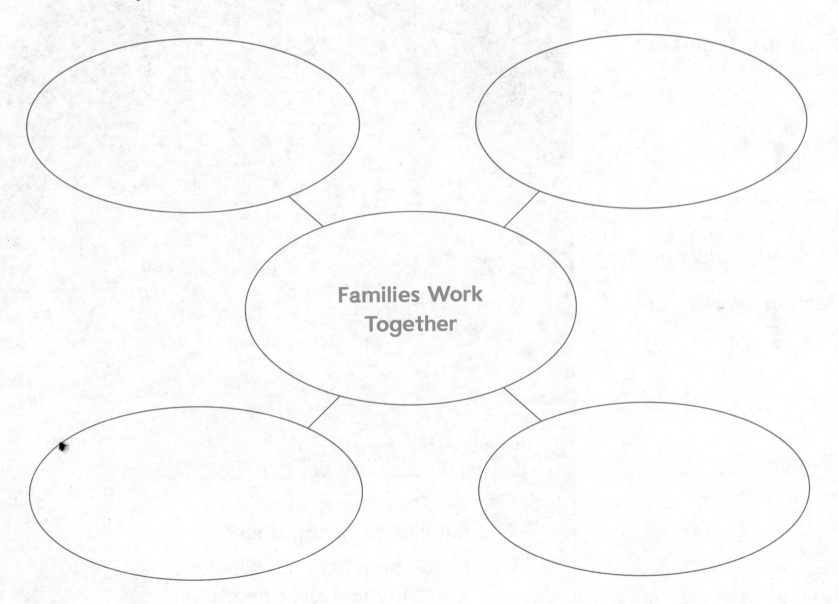

Families Work Together

TIME
FOR KIDS·

TAKE NOTES

Knowing why you are reading a text can help you focus on important details. Write a purpose for reading here.

_____

_____

_____

_____

As you read, make note of:

Interesting Words _____

_____

_____

_____

Key Details _____

_____

_____

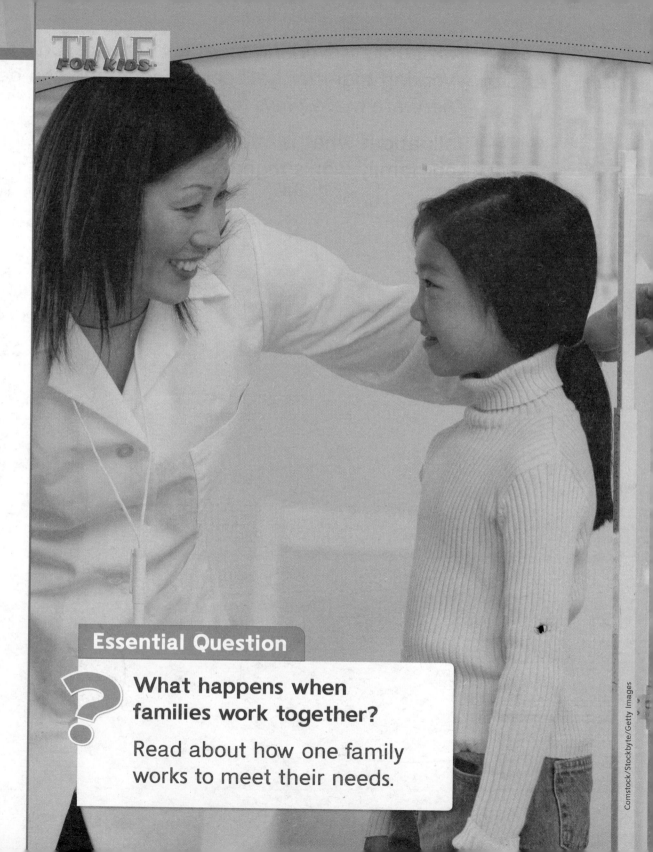

Essential Question

?

What happens when families work together?

Read about how one family works to meet their needs.

Comstock/Stockbyte/Getty Images

Families Work!

Ellen Yung had a busy day at work! She put a cast on a broken arm, used a bandage to cover a deep cut, and helped twenty patients. Ellen is a doctor for children. **Customers** can get sick at any time, so pediatricians work long hours. They have hard **jobs**.

Ellen's husband works long hours, too. Steve is a firefighter. At the firehouse, he makes sure the **tools** work properly. He **checks** the hoses and fire trucks. At the fire, Steve rescues people from hot flames and smoke. The firefighters all work together to put out the fire.

When a fire alarm sounds, Steve suits up quickly.

FIND TEXT EVIDENCE

Read

Paragraph 1

Key Details

Underline details that tell why Ellen had a busy day. Why do doctors like Ellen work long hours?

_____

_____

Paragraph 2

Synonyms

Circle *flames* in the text. Then **circle** a word with almost the same meaning.

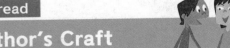

Reread

Author's Craft

How does the author compare the jobs that Ellen and Steve have?

FIND TEXT EVIDENCE

Read

Paragraph 1

Ask and Answer Questions

Ask a question about a way two family members work together.

_____

_____

Underline text evidence that helps you answer it.

Paragraph 2

Key Details

Circle details that tell why the family decides to buy a washing machine.

Reread

Author's Craft

How does the author help you understand the way a family decides to spend their money?

At home, the Yung family works together too. Hanna sets the table for dinner. She also helps wash the dishes. Everyone has weekly **chores**. Mom and Hanna do the dusting and mopping. Dad and her brother, Zac, do the laundry. They wash, dry, and fold the clothes. Mom makes a shopping list each week. She lists items they need and things they want.

A short time ago, Zac wanted a new laptop. The family needed a new washing machine. They could only **spend** money on one item. Both **cost** the same. They had to **choose**. Clean clothes are needed for school and work. A new laptop is nice, but did Zac need it? Ellen and Steve thought about their family's needs. They decided to buy the washing machine.

Hanna's brother, Zac, helps with the meals.

What Are Some Needs and Wants?

Needs	Wants
Water	Skateboard
Food	Video game
Shelter	Basketball
Clothing	

Zac knows that his parents have busy jobs. They bring home money to pay for their needs and wants. They needed that washing machine. Zac still wants a laptop. The family has decided to save some money each week so they can buy it in the future.

Summarize

Use your notes to help you orally summarize the key details in "Families Work!"

FIND TEXT EVIDENCE

Read

Chart

Draw a box around the title of the chart. **Circle** the heading of each column.

Paragraph 1
Key Details
What will the family buy in the future?

_____

_____

Underline text evidence that explains how they will be able to buy it.

Reread

Author's Craft

Why does the author show the two photographs with the chart?

(l)McGraw-Hill Education/Ken Karp;(r)C Squared Studios/Photodisc/Getty Images

Vocabulary

Talk with a partner about each word. Then answer the questions.

checks

Mom **checks** the car tires before a trip.

Who checks the mailbox in your family?

_____

_____

choose

Raul will **choose** a book to read to the class.

What will you choose to read today?

_____

_____

> **Build Your Word List** **Draw a box** around the word *save* on page 67. Use a word web to write more forms of the word in your writer's notebook. You may use a dictionary to help you.

chores

One of my **chores** is to feed our dog.

What is one of your chores?

_____

_____

cost

We bought a book that did not **cost** a lot of money.

What is a gift that doesn't cost a lot of money?

_____

_____

customers

Many **customers** visited the new store.

What can customers buy at a supermarket?

_____

_____

jobs
Nurse and doctor are two **jobs** at a hospital.

What are two jobs at a school?

_____

_____

spend
Greg decided to **spend** his money on a game.

What are two things families spend their money on?

_____

_____

tools
My mother used **tools** to fix my brother's bicycle.

What is a tool you saw an adult use?

_____

_____

Synonyms

Synonyms are words that have almost the same meaning. *Big* and *large* are synonyms.

FIND TEXT EVIDENCE

On page 66, I read that Mom "lists items they need and things they want." In this sentence, items *and* things *are synonyms. I see that items are things on a list.*

She lists items they need and things they want.

Your Turn Use a print or digital thesaurus to write a synonym for the word below.

jobs, page 67 _____

_____

hana/Datacraft/Getty Images

Ask and Answer Questions

When you read, asking questions helps you think about parts of the text you may have missed or do not understand well.

🔍 FIND TEXT EVIDENCE

As I read the last paragraph on page 66, I ask myself, "Why did the family decide to buy a washing machine instead of a laptop?"

> Page 66
>
> A short time ago, Zac wanted a new laptop. The family needed a new washing machine. They could only spend money on one item. Both cost the same. They had to choose.

When I reread to answer my question, I understand the family could only buy one of the things. The family had to make a choice.

Your Turn Think of a question you have about the selection. Reread the parts of the text that will help you answer your question.

_____

_____

_____

Charts

"Families Work!" is an expository text. It gives facts and information about a topic. It can have text features, such as photographs with captions and charts.

FIND TEXT EVIDENCE

I can tell that "Families Work!" is expository text because it gives facts about how family members work to meet their needs. It also has text features.

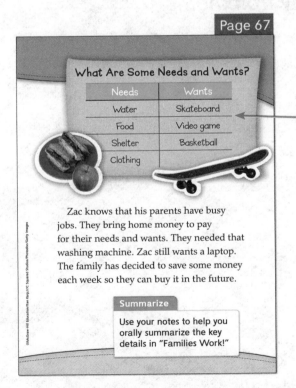

Page 67

What Are Some Needs and Wants?

Needs	Wants
Water	Skateboard
Food	Video game
Shelter	Basketball
Clothing	

Zac knows that his parents have busy jobs. They bring home money to pay for their needs and wants. They needed that washing machine. Zac still wants a laptop. The family has decided to save some money each week so they can buy it in the future.

Summarize

Use your notes to help you orally summarize the key details in "Families Work!"

Chart

A chart shows information in an organized way that is easy to see. Facts may be in rows and columns.

Your Turn How does the author show information in the chart?

_____

_____

_____

_____

Key Details

Key details are important pieces of information in a text. Key details can be found in the text and photographs of a selection.

🔍 **FIND TEXT EVIDENCE**

As I read and look at the photos on pages 64 and 65 of "Families Work!" I understand that Ellen Yung works as a pediatrician, or a doctor for kids. Her husband, Steve, works as a firefighter. They both work away from home.

> **Detail**
>
> (Page 65)
>
>
> Ellen is a pediatrician, and Steve is a firefighter.

 Your Turn Continue reading "Families Work!" Then fill in the graphic organizer with key details.

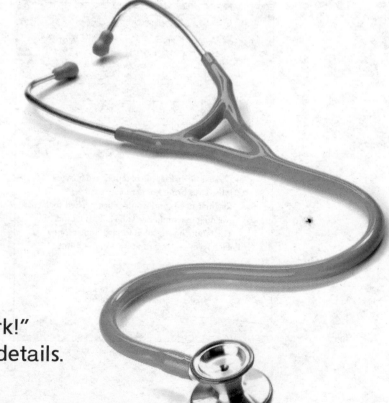

Detail	Detail	Detail
(Page 65)		

Ellen is a pediatrician, and Steve is a firefighter.

Respond to Reading

COLLABORATE Talk about the prompt below. Think about how the author presents details and important information. Use your notes and graphic organizer.

How does the author show how families work and make choices about spending the money they earn?

_____

_____

_____

_____

_____

_____

_____

_____

_____

Interview

You can find out information by asking a person questions in an **interview**. Suppose you want to learn how someone spends money. You could ask: *What is your favorite thing to buy?*

What other interview questions could you ask?

_____

_____

When you conduct an interview, take careful notes on the responses to your questions.

Job Description Sheet With a partner, interview someone who has a job that interests you. Then create a job description sheet with drawings or photos. Write captions or sentences describing the pictures you show.

Choose the person you will interview:

_____

Discuss questions you may ask about his or her job.

Families Working Together

 How does the author help you understand what Mary and her mom do on Tuesdays in the summer?

Literature Anthology: pages 60–63

Talk About It Reread page 61. Why do you think the author begins the selection with the time?

Cite Text Evidence Answer the questions about the trip Mary and her mom make with details from the text.

Where do they go?	What do they do?	What does Mary say?

Write The author helps me understand what Mary and

her mom do on Tuesdays _____

_____

_____

? **How does the author use text features to help you understand who consumers are?**

Talk About It Look at the text features on pages 62 and 63. Talk about what the sidebar and photographs tell about consumers.

Cite Text Evidence Write three ways that text features help you understand what consumers are.

Sidebar Text	Chart	Photographs

Write The text features help me understand what

consumers are by _____

_____

_____

Quick Tip

Use the sentence starters to talk about the text.

The text in the sidebar explains...

The chart shows...

The photos and captions...

Evaluate Information

How do the Gelders earn money with the fresh fruit they do not sell?

Respond to Reading

COLLABORATE

Discuss the prompt below. Be sure to use evidence from the text and the text features to answer the question.

How does the author organize information to show how a family farm produces food for consumers?

_____

_____

_____

_____

_____

_____

_____

Why We Work

Literature Anthology:
pages 64-65

Look around you. The things you see have been produced, or made by a person at work. These things are called goods.

Some people have jobs that provide or offer services. Services are actions that people do.

Reread the page. In paragraph 1, **underline** a sentence that helps you understand the meaning of *goods* in the text. In paragraph 2, **circle** the sentence that tells the meaning of *services*.

Does the photograph show people producing goods or providing a service? Explain your answer.

_____

_____

_____

COLLABORATE

Discuss how the author compares the work people do. Use vocabulary from the selection.

Some service jobs include a teacher or a food server. A teacher provides the service of helping students learn. A food server brings food to your table at a restaurant.

There are jobs that provide services that keep people healthy and safe.

When people make goods or provide services, they earn money. They can use the money to buy more goods and services that cost money. People who buy things are consumers.

Workers in factories produce goods like cars that people buy.

Reread paragraph 1. **Circle** the examples the author uses to describe service jobs. **Draw a box** around details that describe the services.

Reread paragraph 2. **Underline** details that tell what workers can do with the money they earn. How are workers also consumers?

_____

_____

_____

_____

_____

_____

COLLABORATE

Discuss why the author describes jobs people do before explaining that these people are also consumers.

Photographs and Captions

Authors can use photos to help you understand the text. Captions are the words that tell about the photos. Not all photographs in an expository text have captions.

FIND TEXT EVIDENCE

Reread the text on page 79. Then look at the photograph. Think about what the author wants to show in the photograph. What goods are the people making in the photograph?

_____

_____

_____

Your Turn Look at the photographs and reread the captions on page 80. How does the author use the photographs to help you understand the text?

_____

_____

Quick Tip

When you look at photographs and read captions, think about details in the text the author wants to show.

? **What have you learned from the selections and the photograph about families working together?**

Talk About It Look at the photograph and read the caption. Talk with a partner about what the family members are doing.

Cite Text Evidence **Circle** details in the photo and caption that show how the family feels when they do work together.

Write The selections I read and this photograph help me understand how families

_____

_____

_____

_____

_____

_____

_____

Quick Tip

Describe what you see in the photograph. Use these sentence starters.

The family is...

Each family member is...

The family looks...

This family enjoys washing the car on a sunny day.

Phrasing and Accuracy

Phrasing is reading groups of words together to sound like talking. Reading with accuracy is reading without making mistakes. Some texts with difficult words and ideas may take reading several times before you can read them with accuracy and phrasing.

Page 66

A short time ago, Zac wanted a new laptop. The family needed a new washing machine. They could only spend money on one item. Both cost the same. They had to choose.

 As you read, ask yourself: Does that sound right? Does that make sense?

Your Turn Go back to page 65.

Take turns reading the page with a partner. If a word is unfamiliar, try to figure it out. Ask whether the word sounds right and makes sense. Then reread the page to your partner focusing on phrasing and accuracy. Complete these sentences.

I was able to _____

Next time I will _____

Quick Tip

As you read, circle words that you do not know or understand. Look for clues in the text and illustrations about their meaning.

Tech Tip

Use an online dictionary to listen to unfamiliar words and learn how to pronounce them.

*Literature Anthology:
pages 60-63*

Expert Model

Features of an Expository Essay

An expository essay is a kind of expository text.

- It gives facts about the topic.

- It has a concluding statement or section.

Word Wise

The author uses the names of family members. The names help readers understand what each person does and how the members of the family work together.

Analyze an Expert Model Studying "Families Working Together" will help you learn to write an expository essay. Reread page 61. Answer the questions below.

Why does the author begin the text with a question?

_____

_____

How does the author show the way Mary feels about selling the food her family grows?

_____

_____

_____

Plan: Brainstorm

Generate Ideas You will write an expository essay about a person who works for the community. Use this space for your ideas. Brainstorm ideas about community workers that interest you. Write or draw your ideas.

Plan: Choose Your Topic

Writing Prompt Write an expository essay that explains what a community worker does. Complete these sentences to help you get started.

My community worker is _____

I think this job is important because _____

_____

I will get information about this worker by _____

_____

Purpose and Audience Authors may write to teach others about their communities. Think about why you chose your topic. Then explain your purpose for writing in your writer's notebook.

Digital Tools
To learn about how to identify your purpose and audience, watch "Purpose of Informative Writing." Go to **my.mheducation.com**.

Plan: Research

Develop Questions Authors may write questions they want to answer in an expository essay. Read an author's questions in the web below. Write two more questions about being a firefighter.

Quick Tip

Use words such as *who, what, where, when, why,* and *how* as you write questions about a community worker.

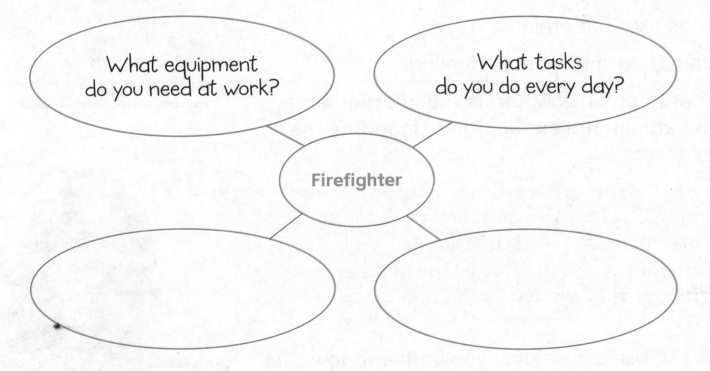

Plan In your writer's notebook, make a web like the one above for your topic. Write questions that you will answer in your essay.

Draft

COLLABORATE

Sentence Types and Lengths

Writers use long and short sentences to make their writing interesting and easy to read. They also use different types of sentences to add interest.

- A **statement** gives information.

- A **question** asks something.

- An **exclamation** shows strong feelings.

Read the paragraph below. **Circle** the question and **draw a box** around the exclamation. **Underline** the longer sentences.

> The family gets up early, and they work for many hours. What foods do they sell? They sell fruits and vegetables. They are so delicious! One popular food is strawberries, so they plant a lot of them.

Write a Draft Use information you gathered to write a draft. Include different types of sentences. Try to use both short and longer sentences in your draft.

Revise

Details Authors add details, such as facts, to help readers understand ideas. Read the text below about Steve Yung's work as a firefighter. Revise the text with details from page 65 that tell more about his work.

> Steve is a firefighter. He works at the firehouse. His job is to
>
> rescue people and put out fires.

_____

_____

_____

_____

 Revise It's time to revise your draft. Make sure to include details that help readers understand what the person does and why this work is important to the community.

Revise: Peer Conferences

Review a Draft Listen carefully as a partner reads his or her work aloud. Begin by telling what you like about the draft. Make suggestions that you think will make the writing stronger.

Partner Feedback Write one of your partner's suggestions that you will use in the revision of your text.

Based on my partner's feedback, I will _____

_____

_____

After you finish giving each other feedback, reflect on the peer conference. What was helpful? What might you do differently next time?

_____

_____

Revision Use the Revising Checklist to help you figure out what text you may need to move, add to, or delete. Remember to use the rubric on page 93 to help you with your revision.

✔ **Revising Checklist**

☐ Does my essay give facts about the community worker?

☐ Does it answer my questions about the community worker?

☐ Do I make a concluding statement?

☐ Are there different sentence types and lengths?

Edit and Proofread

When you **edit** and **proofread**, you look for and correct mistakes in your writing. Rereading a revised draft several times will help you catch any errors. Use the checklist below to edit your sentences.

Tech Tip

If you type your essay, remember to use the "tab" key to indent the first word of each paragraph.

✔ Editing Checklist

☐ Do all sentences begin with a capital letter and end with a punctuation mark?

☐ Are all the words spelled correctly?

☐ Are commas used correctly?

☐ Are all sentences complete sentences?

☐ Is the conjunction *and* used correctly to combine sentences?

Grammar Connections

Make sure you used commas to separate three or more items in a series.

I used the colors red, white, and blue in my poster.

List two mistakes you found as you proofread your text.

1 _____

_____

2 _____

_____

Publish, Present, and Evaluate

Publishing Create a neat, clean final copy of your expository text. As you write your draft, be sure to print neatly and legibly. You may add illustrations or other visuals to make your published work more interesting.

Presentation Practice your presentation when you are ready to present your work. Use the Presenting Checklist to help you.

Evaluate After you publish and present your expository text, use the rubric on the next page to evaluate your writing.

✔ **Presenting Checklist**

☐ Sit up or stand up straight.

☐ Look at different people in the audience.

☐ Speak slowly and clearly.

☐ Speak loudly so that everyone can hear you.

☐ Answer questions using facts from your essay.

1 What did you do successfully? _____

_____

_____

2 What needs more work? _____

_____

_____

Listening When you listen actively, you pay close attention to what you hear. When you listen to other students' presentations, take notes to help you better understand their ideas.

What I learned from ....'s presentation:

_____

Questions I have about ....'s presentation:

_____

✔ **Listening Checklist**

☐ Make eye contact with the speaker.

☐ Use body language that shows you are listening.

☐ Decide which facts are important.

☐ Think about what the speaker does well.

☐ Think of questions you can ask.

4	3	2	1
• uses specific facts about a community worker's job	• tells information about a community worker's job	• uses information that does not relate to the topic	• most information is not based on facts from sources
• sentences vary in length and type	• sentences are different lengths	• sentences are mostly the same length	• sentence length is the same
• has a clear statement or paragraph that concludes the essay	• has a concluding statement	• does not have a clear conclusion	• does not have a concluding statement
• is free or almost free of errors	• has few errors	• has many errors that distract from the meaning of the essay	• has many errors that make the essay hard to understand

Spiral Review

You have learned new skills and strategies in Unit 1 that will help you to read and understand texts. Now it is time to practice what you have learned.

- **Inflectional Endings**
- **Synonyms**
- **Key Details**
- **Character, Setting, Events**
- **Beginning, Middle, End**
- **Charts**

Connect to Content

- **Folktale Book Report**
- **Respond to the Read Aloud**
- **Technology Chart**

Read the selection and choose the best answer to each question.

COMMUNITY HEROES

1 Many firefighters do not get paid for their work. They are volunteers. They may work at other jobs to make money. Their work as firefighters is a gift to their community.

2 Volunteer firefighters work hard to keep the towns safe. They go through many hours of training. They get called to help people at all hours of the day and night. Some can be as young as eighteen. Some are as old as eighty.

3 Volunteers face the same dangers as other firefighters do. They do more than just put out fires. They help at car crashes. They save people caught in flood waters. They hurry to help people who become sick or hurt at home.

4   These special helpers are part of a team. One person drives the truck. Others put up the ladder. Some hold the hose that sprays water on a fire. They help each other stay safe. The teams are like families. Some stations even have dogs.

5   Volunteer firefighters like helping their neighbors. The community helps them, too. People give money for trucks and tools. They take food to the firehouse. They thank firefighters for their important work. In this way, firefighters and community members work together to keep communities safe.

Volunteers Help Communities	Communities Help Volunteers
put out fires	give money for trucks and tools
help after car crashes	take food to the firehouse
help during floods	thank firefighters for their work

(t)kaiskynet/Shutterstock.com; (b) Eric Isselee/Shutterstock.com

SHOW WHAT YOU LEARNED

1 Why is the work of volunteer firefighters a kind of gift?

A The firefighters have other types of jobs.

B The firefighters do not get paid for their work.

C The firefighters help with burning houses.

D The firefighters face many kinds of danger.

2 Paragraph 3 is important to the passage because it —

F tells about how firefighter teams are like families

G shows that the firefighters do more than put out fires

H gives details about how firefighters are trained

J explains how firefighters help during floods

3 Which word in paragraph 4 means the same as volunteers?

A helpers

B others

C teams

D families

4 The chart helps the reader understand —

F why some people become volunteers for their communities

G who can become a volunteer firefighter in a community

H why some communities cannot pay their firefighters

J how volunteers and their communities help each other

> **Quick Tip**
>
> Look for important details that give information about the main idea. Ask yourself questions that begin with *Who? What? Where? When? Why?* and *How?* The answers help you find key details.

Read the selection and choose the best answer to each question.

If Squirrels were Rabbits

[1]   A great storm was coming. Crow had warned the forest animals. He said the wind would bend trees. It would snap the branches.

[2]   The squirrels met under an oak tree. They were afraid. Their nests were high in the trees. What would happen to their homes?

[3]   A young squirrel named Flit spoke up. He said if squirrels were rabbits they would be safe. Their homes would be deep in the ground. Flit thought the squirrels should ask the rabbits to help them dig holes.

[4]   An older squirrel shook his head. He said that squirrels and rabbits were no longer friends. He could not remember why this was so.

[5] Flit sneaked across the creek to Rabbit Village later that day. A group of rabbits saw him coming. Flit stopped a few feet from them. He took a deep breath. Then he asked if they would help the squirrels get ready for the storm.

[6] The biggest rabbit hopped closer to Flit. He said that rabbits and squirrels had been enemies for many years. He could not remember why this was so.

[7] The rabbit returned to the others. They spoke in low <u>voices</u>. Then the big rabbit hopped back to Flit. He said they would help the squirrels. He told Flit that when animals forget why they are enemies, they should be friends.

1 Flit thinks that the squirrels should —

   A show the rabbits how to build nests in the trees

   B stay under the ground during the storm

   C run away from the storm

   D sneak into Rabbit Village

2 In paragraph 7, the word <u>voices</u> means —

   F in a loud voice

   G listening to one voice

   H more than one voice

   J without a voice

3 By the end of the story, how have the feelings of the rabbits changed?

   A They remember why rabbits and squirrels are enemies.

   B They believe that Flit is not telling the truth.

   C They think that rabbits should not help squirrels.

   D They decide that rabbits and squirrels should be friends.

> **Quick Tip**
>
> When you are not sure of a word's meaning, look for word parts such as the endings -s and -ed. Take off the ending and see if you recognize a familiar word.

Focus on Genre

Reread the story *Help! A Story of Friendship* on pages 36–57 of the **Literature Anthology**.

• Why do you think the author chose to use animals in this story?

_____

_____

_____

• How does the illustration on page 48 show that this is a fantasy story?

_____

_____

_____

Talk about how one or more parts of the story could not be possible in real life. Then complete the Graphic Organizer on page 101 to show details that prove *Help! A Story of Friendship* is a fantasy story.

Detail	Detail	Detail

Synonyms

Synonyms are words with meanings that are alike. You can use a dictionary to help you figure out if two words are synonyms.

Look up the definition of each word listed below the word bank. Use the definition to choose a synonym from the word bank. Write the synonym on the line.

| plead | actions | chores | checks |

movements _____

beg_____

examines _____

duties_____

Put the words from the word bank in alphabetical order in your writer's notebook. Know that sometimes you will need to look to the second or third letter.

Write a Book Report

COLLABORATE

A book report has your opinion on something you read. With a partner, find an example of a book report online or in print. Fill in the information from the book report:

Title: _____

Main characters: _____

Main events: _____

_____

Opinion and reasons: _____

_____

Write a book report about a popular folktale you find in a library or online. Make notes as you read the folktale.

- Name the characters and retell important events.

- Give your opinion. Do you like the folktale or not?

- Support your opinion with reasons or examples.

- Draw a picture of an event or character in the folktale.

- Conclude with a final sentence about the folktale.

Respond to the Read Aloud

The main events in a story are what happens in the beginning, middle, and end. It's important to follow the events in order to understand the characters and what happens in the story.

Listen to "The New Kid."

Describe the main events.

Write about the main events in the beginning, middle, and end of the story.

> ### Quick Tip
>
> Listen carefully to words that help show you the order of the story such as *then*, *next*, and *after*.

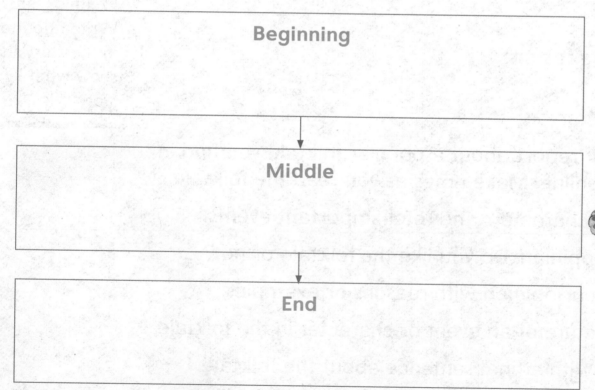

Beginning

Middle

End

Laura Gonzalez

Technology Chart

Create a chart that lists a type of technology your family uses for communication, transportation, or for fun. The chart should include how this technology changed people's lives. Use print or online resources to help you learn more. Look at the chart below as an example.

Technology	How It Changed People's Lives
Communication: cell phone	People can easily get in touch with each other.

- First, list some types of technology your family uses.

- Circle items on your list that are used for communication, transportation, or fun.

- Choose one of the items for your chart.

- Draw the chart and fill in the information.

Share the information on your chart with a partner. Discuss other technology your family uses. Do you think using technology is always better? Why or why not?

Chiyo Hoshikawa/amanaimagesRF

TRACK YOUR PROGRESS

What Did You Learn?

Use the rubric to evaluate yourself on the skills that you learned in this unit. Circle your scores below.

	excellent	good	fair	needs work
Inflectional Endings	4	3	2	1
Synonyms	4	3	2	1
Key Details	4	3	2	1
Character, Setting, Events	4	3	2	1
Beginning, Middle, End	4	3	2	1
Charts	4	3	2	1

What is something you want to get better at?

_____

_____

Text to Self Think about the texts you read in this unit. Tell your partner about a personal connection you made to one of the texts. Use the sentence starter to help you.

I made a connection to . . . because . . .

RESEARCH AND INQUIRY

Present Your Work

With your group, plan how you will present your job description sheet to the class. Discuss the sentence starters below and write your answers.

Ann the Mail Carrier

Ann delivers the mail. The community needs her. Her job earns money for her family.

Mail Carrier

The part of the sheet I will present is _____

_____

I will explain how the words and pictures in the sheet

go together: _____

_____

Quick Tip

Decide in which order to present the information in your sheet. This will help you make sure that everyone has a chance to share their part of the presentation.

Presenting Checklist

- ☐ Listen when someone else in your group is speaking.
- ☐ Be ready to speak when it is your turn to present.
- ☐ Point to your part of the sheet.
- ☐ Speak clearly and in complete sentences.